THE WOMAN'S PLAYBOOK

A SIMPLE GUIDE TO FINDING THE COMMITTED AND LOVING MAN YOU HAVE ALWAYS DESERVED

Table of Contents

Introduction

Do you suffer in relationships, and always go for the wrong guy?

Do the men you want to notice you, pay you no attention at all?

Does love seem to do you no favours, no matter how hard you try?

If this sounds like you, then you need to make *The Woman's Playbook* your bible, because it is going to teach you everything you need to know to help you get the man you really deserve.

Relationships can seem like a minefield. Every step you take in what seems to be the right direction just blows up in your face. You find yourself constantly back at square one, asking what you did in all of your past lives to deserve this rotten luck in love. But you *must* stop beating yourself up!

Blaming yourself, the universe, or even all the men you have ever been involved with, is not going to make any difference to your love life. Instead you need to pay close attention to what you are about to read. If love is a game, then you need *The Woman's Playbook* to teach you the rules!

This guide is designed to open your eyes and show you your true potential, and remind you of what you have to offer in a relationship. Once you realize how special you are, you will stop going for the wrong men; *the men who mess you about and make you feel worthless and hopeless*, and you will be able to define and recognize the kind of man who is going to appreciate you, and make you happy.

The first section of this guide will teach you what men are looking for in a woman, and how you can use what you already have to attract the *right* man for you. It will tell you what the desirable traits of a woman are, give you tips on how to find the right man, provide instructions on how to get his attention and establish your compatibility, and guide you to achieve success on your first date.

Once you have defined who the right kind of man for you is, got his attention, and succeeded in having a fabulous first date, the second section of this guide will then share the secrets of how to keep your guy hooked and wanting more! It will teach you how to change your behavior in the subtlest of ways to entice your new lover, and make him realize that you are '*the one*'.

You will learn that confidence is key, and find out how you can take hold of the reigns in your growing relationship, and get exactly where you want to be. You will also find out how to avoid the dreaded *friends zone*; discover whether or not you are really *girlfriend material*; and discover how to know when it is the right time to get serious and move your relationship into the bedroom and beyond.

The final section of this book will lay out all the common mistakes that women everywhere make in relationships, and make sure that you don't fall into the same traps and end up pushing your man away. With key tips on helping you to figure out if your guy really is Mr. Right; and if he is, further tips on how you can avoid common mistakes *like the plague,* you will feel confident in getting him to commit and fall in love with you, so that you can both settle down happily, and build a future together.

Good luck in achieving happiness… and always remember that you're worth it!

Section 1

Find The Right Man

What Are The Traits of a Desirable Woman?

So you have been in the dating game for "X" amount of years, and yet you always find yourself back where you started… *back to square one*… single, heartbroken, and feeling like maybe you should just give up, get a cat and accept your spinster fate.

Snap out of your miserable bubble immediately! It is not attractive, and it is *not* going to help get you your Mr. Right. People who wallow in their misery never get what they really want. Those who stand up and fight for their right to be happy, do!

I know what you are thinking, it's not as easy as it sounds and you've tried your best, but you seem to be cursed in matters of love. *Sound the violins.* I do understand, dating is not easy, and the competition is fierce out there, but you can't give up. All you need is a new perspective, and that is what *The Woman's Playbook* is here to give you.

What makes a woman attractive?

You might think that men are attracted to women who have sexy bodies, perfect skin, luscious hair and a face full of make-up. You might even think that you have to be either be incredibly intelligent and beautiful, or a porn star in the bedroom to be lucky enough to get hold of a gorgeous man and keep him for any significant length of time.

It is true that men are initially drawn to beauty, intelligence and great sex. *I mean who wouldn't be?* But I'd like to suggest that these qualities in a woman actually make it more difficult for them to succeed in finding the *right guy,* and developing a long-term relationship with them.

For a start these kinds of women are attracting men, who to be honest, don't seem very difficult to attract. To me this suggests that they probably aren't going to be the most committed type of guy, seeing as his head is going to turn every time a beautiful, intelligent or sexy woman comes into his line of vision! Is this the sort of man you want to be with?

I'm not saying he will be unfaithful, but his natural male instincts might be enough to cause your own insecurity to shoot up and through the ceiling - and jealous girlfriends are never attractive I'm afraid! Beauty, intelligence and sex appeal are not necessarily the things that are going to guarantee you your dream relationship.

Anyway - What about all of the ordinary girls out there?

There are many geeky girlfriends who seem to be in happy and content relationships; and many introverted women, women with not-so-perfect bodies, and women who aren't particularly intelligent but like to have a giggle and watch really bad TV with their partners, cuddled up on the sofa at the weekends, who have found men that love them and are willing to commit. So what is it about *these* girls that men find attractive?

Let me share a little secret with you...

All men are going to be physically attracted to the hot, beautiful and intelligent women out there in the world, and there is nothing that is ever going to change that, whether they own up to it or not; but what guy really wants is a woman he is one hundred per cent compatible with, who he can be himself around, who makes him feel amazing and comfortable and content. When a man is looking for a relationship, he isn't looking for a model girlfriend; he is looking for someone who is real, a girl who is confident within her self, and who will be a friend and a proper life companion.

The great news is that *any woman*, no matter who you are or what you look like, has the ability to be the perfect girlfriend for a man they are truly compatible with.

If you concentrate on being the best version of YOU, then you are more likely to attract a man who will be right for YOU. He will be attracted to the traits you are displaying because he has things in common with you and can relate to them. And remember that every man is different, so there is absolutely no point in trying to be someone you are not in order to attract "men", because all men are attracted to different things in a woman.

How to discover your own unique attractive traits

If you want to find a man who is right for you, then you must first work on understanding and maximizing the potential of your own desirability. Every woman has her own set of inner and outer attractive characteristics. Once you can recognize what yours are, and more importantly *accept* your own attractive features, *or what you probably perceive as flaws*, then you will be able to exude an inner confidence which is like an aphrodisiac to the right guy!

The problem of course, is that most women resist the things about themselves that could be working towards attracting the right guy. What you need to do is start *embracing* your flaws, and make them work *for* you rather than against you.

Complete the following steps to discover your own unique attractive traits:

1. Make two lists – one list should be all of the **physical** things you like about yourself. Try to include the things you feel make you unique, special and attractive; like the way your hair curls only at the ends and makes you feel feminine, or how amazing you look and feel in red lippy. The other list should be all of the things you like about your **personality.** Include things like how you enjoy organizing events and people, or the fact that you can make new friends quickly, or that you are great with young children.

2. Now ask the same two questions to as many people who know you that you can think of. *Don't be shy*, you can tell them it is a work-related self-improvement exercise that everyone at your company has been asked to take part in. They don't need to know what you are really trying to do.

Results:

You may be surprised at some of the positive things people say about you! For example, perhaps several people have mentioned how attractive they find the shape of your hooked nose? Or maybe what you perceive about yourself to be bossy, others might view as assertiveness.

Have a long hard think about every single feature that has been mentioned in this exercise, because *these* are the things that define the way other people see you, and the way you see yourself – They are your *desirable traits* as a woman, so it is best to acknowledge, accept, and start embracing all of the things you thought made you unattractive.

You must learn to love yourself if you want a man to love you too - *even all the things you thought were your flaws!*

Finding The Right Man

Once you have embraced who you are as a woman, and I mean *truly* accepted all of your perceived flaws as attractive traits that make you who you are, then suddenly you will be on track to attracting a man. But not just any man – *the right man* – and there *is* a difference!

You will of course attract a variety of different men at this stage, because confidence is *sexy*. You should now be glowing with a new sense of 'self' that is like a neon flashing arrow pointing at you and saying – *Look! This woman is naturally gorgeous and available!* It is up to you to wade through this sea of opportunity to find Mr. Right, and hopefully, with your newfound sense of self-worth you should be able to do just that.

Finding the right man is all about knowing what you deserve, and also knowing yourself. Successful relationships are based on compatibility, and choosing the right man *for you* means being honest with yourself about how compatible you really are with the men you are choosing. This can be a challenge when all of a sudden you are attracting the attention of the kind of men that make you go weak at the knees.

Be careful! There is a reason that many women have several failed relationships under their belts; and that reason is *incompatibility*. I'm not saying that failed relationships are a bad thing; on the contrary, they can all be counted as learning experiences. But sooner or later, a woman is going to get fed up of falling in love and having her heart broken, and she is going to pick up a book like this, in desperation, and silently scream – *What am I doing wrong*? Are you that woman?

Learn from your past relationships

Let's take a look at all of your past relationships. Think about what was good about each one, and how they all went up in smoke. Look for recurring themes, analyze your own behavior, and look for signs that show where you and your ex-partners were incompatible.

The only way you will learn and move forward is if you can analyze your own past experiences and learn from your mistakes. That is what old relationships are there for. They are not there as a constant taunt, sneering at you and reminding you that you are hopeless in love; they are there to show you how to improve yourself and your future relationships with men, so use them!

Try this…

If you are on friendly terms with your past partners, maybe it could help if you talk to them? Sometimes we can go through a whole lifetime, never really knowing the whole truth about the experience that the other people in our past relationships have had, because we were so absorbed in how *we* were feeling during those times. If you are lucky enough to be able to talk to your ex-partners now though, you can gain some really *valuable insight* by asking them to share their poropectives with you.

A good way to approach this sort of conversation is to direct it towards certain things in the relationship that you think are significant. Include happy incidents and difficult times too if you can.

Remember:

Your aim is to learn more about the type of man who is *right for you*; which means you need to look carefully at what kind of a person you are in relationships, as well as what kind of men have been bad for you in the past. Placing blame at someone else's door is never going to teach you anything unless you are able to take some of the responsibility for your choices. I am assuming that you did *choose* to be with these men, after all?

Food for thought...

Maybe you are making the wrong choices, and as a result, perhaps you are not able to be the woman you really are?

For example, have you always played a weaker role in relationships and allowed your partners to take the lead and make decisions? If so, have you ever considered that maybe you are allowing your true self to be suppressed? Maybe what you really need is a man who is able to give you more space and freedom so that you can assert your independence, and be the woman you really are!

I'm sorry to say it, but there are some very needy men out there, and they tend to be the ones who boss their girlfriends around and end up leading them about like the poor women are dogs on the end of a leash. *You are not a dog!* And even if you were, you would still need time off the leash, so that you could run around by yourself in a big open space and feel happy.

On the other hand, maybe you have been too assertive in past relationships, to the point of being bossy or a nag? Is it time you step down off your pedestal and submit to a man with a bigger ego than your own? You can find great fulfillment in discovering an underlying trait to your personality that opposes the character you portray to the world. Some women who have high-powered jobs for instance, enjoy relationships where they can surrender all the important decision-making and responsibility to their partner.

BONUS MATERIAL:
How do you know if he is the right man for you?

Deciding whether a man is right for you before you have even been on the first date is somewhat presumptuous, don't you think? But you do want to feel confident that you aren't wasting your time on a man who is completely wrong for you, so I have compiled a checklist to help you think about how much time to spend chasing after the man you are currently interested in.

When you find a man attractive it is a common affliction to be able only to see the things you like about them. Women in love are often completely blind to potential incompatibility problems. Try asking yourself these questions, to get you thinking about what kind of man you really want to be with in a long-term relationship…

- **Is he attractive, but modest at the same time?** There is nothing worse than a man who is drop dead gorgeous and knows it. Sure, you may be drawn in by his sexy charm to begin with, but there is nothing worse than being in competition with a man who loves himself more than he loves you. *It will quickly get on your nerves.*

- **Is he caring and considerate?** A man, who demonstrates a certain level of caring for other people in the community or at work, is a keeper. The best boyfriend is a man who puts other people's needs before his own. This is a man who will want to listen to you, and will want to understand how you feel and know what you want from him - *because your needs will be just as important to him as his own*! If you spot the object of your desire helping another individual – *standing up for a pregnant lady on the bus, helping an old man across the road, or picking up a child's toy in the supermarket to hand to it's screaming little owner in* *the trolley* – then you know he is the type of guy to take note of. Also, be observant when you listen to him talking about other people's problems – does he show a healthy level of empathy as well as being practical, or is he overly critical and dogmatic in his approach, and do you get the sense that his opinions are more important to him than the way the person whose problem it is feels?

- **Is he able to provide for you?** A guy doesn't have to be rich to be able to provide for you in a relationship. We are living in modern times and a bread-winning man is not the Holy Grail. I fact many women (and men) would be offended if I suggested that the *right* man is a man who will earn all of the money to provide for the family, while the woman does her maternal thing at home with the house and kids. *No – this is not what I am referring to at all*. What I mean by being able to provide for you is to make sure that the guy is responsible and unselfish in the way he lives his life. If you go for a man who is frivolous with his money, spending large chunks on random flashy adult toys and dipping into his income liberally whenever he feels like splurging, without any sense of the future, then you are more likely to come up against financial difficulties and relationship issues, when he discovers that suddenly his money isn't just his own business any more! Instead, look for a man who is responsible with his cash, and who looks ahead, further than his next paycheck. A man who is generous and sharing is also a keeper.

- **Does he have a good relationship with his mother?** It is important to observe the way a man treats women who are 'above' him in some way. This might mean analyzing his relationship with his mother or other female relative who he is meant to look up to, or taking note of how he talks about his female boss, or big sister. You can tell a lot about a guy from the way he behaves around other women. If the guy you like respects women, then it is probably safe to say that you can look forward to an equal and balanced relationship with him, where issues that arise can be discussed on a calm and rational level.

- **Does he pay attention to the details?** You may not know him very well yet, but if you can find out how closely he pays attention to things and people, then you may be able to figure out whether or not he is going to be the type of person who cares enough about the details in your relationship. It is the little things, like remembering people's birthdays, or how they like their coffee – these seemingly insignificant details can give you insight into how attentive a boyfriend he is likely to be. Every woman wants a man who takes the time to make her feel special, and a man who pays attention, ticks that box!

How To Get His Attention!

Getting a man to notice you is not difficult. I mean, if you wear a banana suit and march down the road with a speakerphone announcing that you're single and looking for Mr. Right, it is going to get you the attention of many potential Mr. Rights, but only the ones who find psychotic banana-clad women attractive are going to show you any interest. On the other hand, if this is the kind of guy you will be most compatible with, *go for it!*

Remember that the bottom line is that you should be aiming to attract a man who is right for *you*.

What I am trying to say though, is that there is no point in going out of your way to get a man's attention if you are not being true to who you are. There are many books that will tell you to use your sexual allure and womanly assets to get men to notice you; and while they may be right in stating that men will notice a woman who wears necklines to accentuate her cleavage, they are wrong in suggesting that these are universal tools that all women possess, and should be using to their own advantage.

Always remember, the key rule when in search for the *right* man is to be one hundred per cent *you*.

So let us explore two simple ways to get a guy to look up and SEE you…

1 A simple splash of color

If you thought that getting a man to notice you in the street, supermarket or at work was just about what you wear, you'd be mistaken. Guys don't pay that close attention to what a girl wears to be honest with you. They may pay more attention if the girl is wearing a tight pair of jeans that shows off her ass perfectly, but I guarantee you it is not the jeans the guy will remember, it is the shape of the woman's bum!

Unless you have a bum you love and want to show it off, don't think too much about the actual outfit. As long as you are wearing something that fits you well and that you feel comfortable in, it is *how* you wear it that the guy will notice – i.e. *with confidence*.

But if you know that you simply aren't the kind of girl who can walk into a room in such a way that everyone will look up at you, focus instead on catching the guy's eye with a vibrant splash of color.

This technique works in a very simple way; the splash of color directly interferes with the guy's range of view, so that even if he isn't looking directly at you, he will have no choice but to see the color in his peripherals, and his gaze will involuntarily move in your direction. Mission accomplished.

Note: It is not *you* he is paying attention to yet; it's just that splash of color he has seen. If you want him to notice *you*, then you will have to anchor his gaze with something else, which we will come onto in a minute.

For now, let's think about some of the things you can use to inject that splash of color onto your person. Here is a list of ideas.

Remember, keep it simple.

- **Wear a large attractive handbag on your shoulder**. It should be all one color, and a color that doesn't clash with everything else you are wearing. Your outfit should be understated and simple to make that splash of color stand out! It is also a good idea to pick a color that suits you, and one that you like. Just make sure that the shade is eye-catching and not a subdued one. **Tip:** A bag that has a shorter strap will work better because the bag will be closer to your face, which means you are more likely to be able to make eye contact too, which is what we will be exploring next.

- **Wear brightly colored, shiny patent or sparkly shoes.** They don't even have to be sexy high heels, they can be flat pumps if you like. The idea is that because they are on your feet, the noticeability of the splash of color or glitz on your feet will be reinforced with movement when you walk past him. **Tip:** As soon as you see him notice your shoes, drop something on the floor so that you have to bend down and pick it up, again giving you the opportunity to make eye contact.

- **Carry something in a vibrant color that you can wave around.** Remember that one single block color works best, and that the color should be eye-catching, like yellow, orange, or lime green. A large notebook or personal organizer will work, or an umbrella if the weather allows. The trick is to use it in a creative way as a kind of flag. You can hold it up and wave it at a bus at the bus stop, or place it on the counter in a coffee shop to get your purse out and pay, and then accidentally shove it off the side onto the floor in the direction of your guy. It might sound a little bit nuts, but this kind of thing really does work, if you are trying to get a guy's initial visual attention.

The main idea is to have fun with fun colors, and give a guy something to look at, it doesn't matter what it is!

2 The all-important eye contact!

There is no point in using the splash of color technique, if you are not going to follow through by drawing him in with a bit of eye contact. It is your job to make him notice *you*, and to make it feel intimate, once your splash of color has caught his visual attention. Otherwise all he has noticed is a big red bag, or a bright purple and green umbrella.

The best way to make the most of eye contact is the simple way – *just smile at him!* You never need a reason to smile at anyone. In fact people should smile at each other more often, but they don't; which actually works in your favour here because it means that your smile will come as a welcome surprise to him.

Tip: Smiling with your mouth open and showing your teeth or gums is more attractive than smiling with your mouth closed, because it shows that you are open-natured and easily approachable. There is also a fun and happy innocence about a girl who smiles with her mouth open, and shows off her teeth. People will warm to you because happiness is contagious. People want to interact with the woman who looks like she is ready to laugh and engage; rather than the woman who skulks in the shadows, maybe offering a suspicious upturned corner of the mouth, but not wanting to get any more involved than that!

Getting a guy's attention doesn't have to be an intricately planned ordeal. Just try to be yourself, and use simple ideas and props that you think will help make you stand out from the crowd.

Finding Common Ground

Once you have offered an open gate for communication, you mustn't let your guy get away! This is your chance to give him a reason to want to get to know you *more*.

So far, you have got his attention and he has seen that you seem to be a friendly and inviting kind of person, but that doesn't necessarily mean that he is suddenly going to take charge and do all of the work. The chances are, he may not even be thinking about the fact that you are interested in getting to know him on a more intimate level; so I'm afraid you are going to have to initiate conversation. Yes, believe it or not, you have to *talk* to the guy if you want to get closer to him.

How do you know whether or not he is interested enough to want to talk to you though? It's pretty scary to go up to someone and just start talking, isn't it? It can be even more terrifying if you already know the guy! Maybe he works in the same work place as you but you haven't ever had the opportunity to get to know each other properly before; or maybe he lives in your block and you share the same lift on occasion?

How do you go from being a complete stranger or awkward acquaintance, to a potential date?

Has a stranger ever chatted you up?

One way to look at it is from his perspective. If you have ever been chatted up by a stranger in a coffee shop, or had to exchange forced conversation with an unfamiliar colleague at the water cooler, then you will know what it feels like to be approached for no apparent reason at all. It's just a bit weird, isn't it? At least it can be, depending on what kind of people you are. So you need to have a valid and relevant reason to talk to him.

For some reason many people have social barriers built up around them that can be difficult to penetrate in public situations. For example, many people go into "coffee shop mode" where they just want to be alone with their paper and latte. Public transport is often another place where people don't generally expect or welcome social interaction with complete strangers.

This doesn't mean that you shouldn't attempt it though, especially as you have already broken down some of those barriers by getting his attention and offering your smile. If he smiles back, take it as a green light!

Ideas to open up conversation

The chances are, you are probably feeling extremely nervous. You are essentially making the first move, with a guy you already kind of want to marry and have kids with - *lots of pressure*! He doesn't know how you feel about him yet though, and you can take advantage of this.

Warning...

As soon as he knows you are head over heels for him, you will have transferred all of the power over to him, which is a bad thing. This is *your* show and *you* should be leading it!

Retain your power by acting like a *normal human being*! Don't treat him like he is anything special, even if you would happily bend down and kiss his feet on request. A guy will sense it if you worship the ground he walks upon, and the loss of a challenge will quickly disinterest him.

Insider information…

Men are quickly seduced when they discover a challenge is nearby. This relates to all things; from fixing a radio, to getting a sexy woman into bed. You can take advantage of a man's natural instinct to chase, hunt down and devour, by *being that challenge*!

So where are we at? You have flagged down his attention with your splash of color, you have drawn him in with an open smile, and now you are going to initiate a proper connection by opening up conversation, but you need to combat the nerves…

Try this…

Imagine, if you will, that he is an old, wrinkly man who has the hots for you! He knows he doesn't stand a chance, but he flirts anyway. Think about how you would behave towards this old man.

You probably wouldn't find him very intimidating for a start, so you certainly wouldn't be nervous. Knowing he fancies you, *even if he is an old man*, is going to give you a confidence boost and make you feel young and beautiful, *in comparison to him anyway!*

Would you be likely to respond to his wicked comments with good-hearted humor? Would you perhaps aim to talk about a topic he can get his teeth into, *even his false gnashes*, if it'll take the attention away from any awkward tension? Unless you are particularly shy, you wouldn't be stuttering your way into a blushing heap of giggles, that's for sure!

If you can bring yourself to see the object of your desire as a *normal human being*, with his own flaws, just like you, then you are more likely to be able to connect with him at this stage. Aim to keep things casual.

Here are some ideas for conversation openers...

- **If he is nearby, ask for his help**. This is a very natural way to open up conversation. You can ask for directions, ask for help opening a really tight bottle lid, or ask for his opinion on something you are both involved in – like watching a football game in the pub. Try to keep your approach relevant to the moment, and neither of you will have any reason to feel awkward or embarrassed.

- **Comment on whatever he is doing**. If you can find a way to involve yourself in whatever he is doing at that moment, you will give him something to talk back to you about. For example, you could comment on a book he is reading. The chances are, you probably haven't read the book, and so commenting on it might feel a bit forced. If you haven't read it, tell him you've been told it's a really good read and that it has been recommended for you to read by a friend, and ask him how he's finding it.

- **Reach for the same thing at the supermarket**. This is a bit cheesy and also takes a bit of quick thinking, but if you are at the supermarket, or any shop, and you see him next to you reaching out for, say a box of cereal or other product, reach out and grab the same one! Firstly it will give you something to laugh about, and secondly it will open up an opportunity for you to communicate with him. You can let him have it and then comment on the fact that you always go for that cereal, and you can both have a rather random, but relevant to the moment conversation about cereal. This is just an example, but you can adapt it to the situation you find yourself in. It doesn't really matter what you talk about, as long as it is relevant to the situation and gives you an opportunity to connect.

- **Offer your name**. It sounds scary, but if you offer your hand to shake and say, "Hi, my name is…" a guy will probably shake your hand on instinct. Just make sure you have something to follow up with. This works best when you are both attending the same event, when you already work in the same environment and haven't ever been properly introduced, or if you are in a social place where talking to strangers is considered normal after eye contact and a smile has been returned, like a bar or nightclub.

- **Give him a compliment.** This tip usually works even better when a guy is on the receiving end, because they are less likely to expect it from a woman. Tell him you like his T-shirt, and maybe ask him where he got it from for a great icebreaker. He will feel good that you noticed, which will make him more receptive to conversation.

The initial icebreaker will always feel terrifying, but as soon as you have made contact, as long as you have thought about the different things you could say, conversation should flow naturally. Normally a guy will make things easier too by leading a conversation once you have opened it up for him, especially if he likes your friendly vibe. Guys tend to be more socially open in public situations than women, because they don't often get hit on in public, and if they do, they would find it flattering rather than an unwanted intrusion.

Just go for it!

The worst that can happen is that he isn't as responsive as you had hoped he would be. At least you can say you tried though, and often the next time you approach him, because you will be a familiar face, he will probably be more responsive then.

From Initiation to First Date

First things first; there's no point in asking a guy out on a date if you don't know whether or not he is interested. Just because a guy has looked at you and returned your smile, it doesn't always mean he finds you attractive or wants to get to know you. He may just be being polite. Don't let this put you off completely though…

You might not be his *type* on the outside; men, like women, can be a bit fickle, but his should never be a deterrent, because often we end up falling in love with people we didn't initially find visually appealing. Attraction is so much more than what a person looks like; it is all about the connection and developing a bond. Attraction is often difficult to explain, because you just feel it or you don't. Did you ever really fancy a hot guy, but when you had a conversation with him, you found yourself feeling disappointed because you didn't feel that essential spark?

In order to find out if there is any chemistry between you, and also to find out whether or not you are likely to be compatible, you must give yourselves the opportunity to find something out about each other. Once you involve yourself in conversation, you should be able to feel whether or not there is potential, and so should he, because you just *know* when you like a person!

What next?

If you have already initiated conversation with your man, it is now time to focus that conversation, in order to establish what you both have in common. If you want to ask him out on a date, you are going to need to give him a reason to say yes. You will do this by *giving* him something to be interested in.

The best way to increase a guy's interest in you is to appeal to his natural sense of curiosity. Even if you haven't managed to establish something concrete that you both have in common – *I mean it can be difficult to find out what someone is really into in such a brief space of time* - you can still pique his interest if you manage to make him feel intrigued about you in some way. Once you have set up the challenge of trying to figure something out about you, then meeting up again is going to be the next inevitable step for him.

How to trigger a man's curiosity

In your first encounter, you need to work hard to find something out about your man that you both have in common. Even the smallest thing can help you get to the next stage in your seduction. Then you need to use this piece of information to trigger his curiosity about you, and then he will want to know more about you.

However, if you aren't able to find anything you have in common, you can side-step this and instead focus on sharing a little something about yourself that sets you apart from other people. Try to include something in your short encounter about yourself that is completely different from what he is expecting. *What is different and unique about you?*

For example;

- **Do you have an unusual sideline job** – like being a nude life-model for student artists? Or are you a writer? Why not take a quick "work-related" call? Fake it or get a friend to call you, and make sure you reveal the quirky details of your secret-life in the telephone conversation for him to overhear. Then when you come off the phone you can say something like "Sorry about that, it was my work!" And if he is interested, he will probably comment or ask questions about what you do! *You will have successfully planted a seed of curiosity.*

- **Do you speak another language?** Take a phone call and speak in your mother tongue, and when you come off the phone he will probably ask about where you are from. A woman who speaks foreign languages is sexy because it gives them an air of mystery and double-life/personality which men find exciting. If you want to add even more quirk, why don't you slip into your foreign language without realizing it, mid-conversation, and then laugh at yourself and translate!

- **Do you have specialist knowledge about anything?** Providing it's not a topic he won't be able to relate to at all, displaying specialist knowledge about something that has come up in your conversation, or that is relevant to the situation, shows that there is more to you than meets the eye. *Who knows, he might just be interested to find out more!* For example, did you ever work as a Barista? If you know a little bit more about coffee than the average person, this could be a useful thing to make evident in a conversation happening in a coffee shop! Men often find random snippets of information interesting, and if you can inject some into the conversation, it might just be enough to make him curious to know what other snippets of information you have to offer!

How do you get that first date?

The trick to getting a first date is to keep this first encounter short and sweet; and leave him wanting more! The way to do this is to give your conversation a limited amount of time, so that you have to wrap it up before he has discovered everything he wants to know about you. When you retain a certain level of mystery and inject a sense of needing to get away or be somewhere, your guy's natural chase instincts will start to kick in.

This doesn't necessarily mean that just because you have said you have an appointment and need to leave, that he is going to ask for your number though. I'm afraid you are going to have to make sure that happens, and here is how...

Firstly you need to interrupt the conversation flow when it has built up enough momentum and you can sense that you have succeeded in engaging your man. You can do this in a number of ways, without making it seem like you need an excuse to get away from him:

1. Set your phone to beep like you have received a text message, and then act disappointed that you have to leave. Your reluctance to go should be subtle though, and refer more to the fact that you're sorry you have to cut the interesting conversation short, than to the fact that you are intensely attracted to him and wish you could chat and gaze into his eyes for hours!

2. Find yourself seized with the realization that you're late for an appointment. Ask him for the time or look at your own watch, and don't forget to apologize for interrupting. Again, your apology doesn't have to be over the top.

3. Be forward, take out your phone and state that you have to go, but that you'd love to meet up and continue talking about whatever it is you are talking about, and then ask for his number. This works especially well if you have mentioned an event you think he might be interested in during your conversation – an exhibition perhaps – and you want to forward him on the details.

Asking a guy out doesn't have to be a terrifying or embarrassing experience if you approach it with a practical mindset instead of an emotional one. The fear is mostly fueled by not wanting to be rejected, but you can practically eliminate that risk by giving the guy a valid reason to want to meet up with you – and that reason doesn't actually have to have anything to do with physical or sexual attraction. You just have to find something interesting to offer. The attraction bit can come later, when you are both more relaxed and have gotten to know each other better.

Remember: The three things to ensure you include in your conversation are…

1. **Relevant small talk** as a means of initiating contact; and establishing something you have in common, or revealing something intriguing about yourself.

2. **A sense of limited time**, so that you can keep it short and sweet, enabling you to promote that sense of urgency so that he is eager to accept your suggestion of exchanging contact details!

3. **A valid reason for him to give you his contact details** – whether it is his number or even an email address.

How to Use Texting To Your Advantage

So you've had a great first date, you're feeling good, and you want to express your enthusiasm with a text... or two... or three...

Before you start gushing about what a great time you had and how funny you think he is, and how you can't wait for the next date... slow down. Slow way down.

Number one, you don't actually know whether your enthusiasm is reciprocated. It might have seemed like he was having the time of his life, and you might have felt like the luckiest girl on the planet, but when you are having a good time yourself, the reality of the situation can become a little blurry. Perhaps you didn't notice him looking at the clock? Perhaps you didn't think much about the excuse he gave to leave early? I don't want to pour cold water on your high, but it's best to be aware of all possibilities, so that you don't end up feeling foolish, or ruining your chances by coming across as too eager.

The first post-date text

The first thing you should do after an amazing date, if you can't handle the anticipation, is send him a simple text message that says thank you for a great time, you enjoyed yourself, and that you'll look forward to hearing from him.

Something along those lines will tell him everything he needs to know, without coming on too strong, and without placing any expectation. Make sure you include the following.

1. **Be polite** – Say thank you for the date, especially if he took you somewhere nice and paid for a few drinks.

2. **Describe your experience** – Tell him you enjoyed the drink, or that it was nice to get to know him a bit better, and that you had fun! Do *not* go overboard and say it was the best experience you have had in years, and that you are so grateful he has lifted you out of your dating slump!

3. **Let him know you'd be happy to repeat the experience** – Men are simple in their approach to women and dating, and they appreciate women who are straightforward too. If you tell him openly that you are open to meeting up again, it will save him a lot of brainwork. Yes, men like to chase women and they like a challenge, but they aren't mind readers, so often they will appreciate when a woman cuts out the game-playing and mixed-messages. The trick is also to keep it sounding casual and open. Do *not* say that you are waiting for his call, or that you have already decided where your second date is going to take place. That would be a bad move. It's always bad to presume.

Leave the ball in his court

Many women will carefully calculate the number of days they should leave to go by before they send the first text, and then spend every minute checking their phone, itching to send it a little bit sooner. I say do it as soon as you feel it is right, even if this is when you get home from your first date, or the next morning.

Don't worry about putting him off or coming across as desperate – it is not the length of time you leave in between your date and your first text that will make you look too eager, it is what you put in the text; and we have already established that you should be open and honest, but also casual, so you should be fine.

The important rule, *if you want a rule*, is to be patient when the ball is not in your court, and responsive but casual and natural when the ball is in your court.

This means that once you have sent your first text, resist sending another the next day to see if he got it! And when he does respond, don't faff about playing hard to get by not texting for another three days even though you are practically bursting at the seams to get things moving. If you play these sorts of games you will only stress yourself out, and he may assume you aren't that interested.

What if he doesn't reply at all?

Don't freak out! Just because he hasn't replied to your first text, it doesn't necessarily mean that he had an awful time and doesn't want to hear from you again. There are a number of potential reasons he hasn't replied, and most of them will have nothing to do with you.

To put your mind at ease, here are some common reasons why guys don't text back…

- They were multi-tasking when they received your message, and once they skim-read it, they deleted it meaning to respond after they had finished doing what they were doing, but then they got distracted by something else and forgot.

- They have been very, very busy, with much more important things. Don't be offended, life tends to have a way of intervening.

- They really enjoyed themselves too but are nervous about asking you out again. Remember, you were probably the one who asked him out the first time! Maybe they don't know what to suggest for a second date?

- They had a great time but they're fresh out of an intense relationship and want to take things slowly.

- Your text has just slipped his mind for the time being.

- He doesn't have much experience in relationships and has been given some ill advice from his mates to play hard to get and keep you hanging for more than a week!

- He has fallen ill and hasn't been well enough to respond.

- A major life event is taking place and he has been distracted by it. For example, a promotion at work, a death in the family, the launch of a new computer game...

Don't take any of these things personally.

How to re-establish contact without appearing needy

The good news is that there are tricky ways you can take the ball back without it seeming like you are desperate for a second date. If you have given him a decent amount of time to respond to your first text, but you haven't heard anything, then feel free to reach out in one of the following ways.

Note...

A good length of time to leave it is just under two weeks. Any less and you won't have given him sufficient time to reply of his own accord, and any longer you may risk losing the spark and momentum from the first date.

- Contact him to see if he wants to come to an event with you that takes place soon! The event will be a valid reason to reach out, despite not hearing back from him, especially if it is something that was mentioned during your first date, or relates to something you know he is interested in. This is a clever tactic that also preserves your vulnerability, because you have made the second date about your mutual interests rather than your feelings for each other. So even if he hasn't quite figured out what he feels for you yet, he will still feel safe to accept the second date, because there is no pressure to express any feelings, or acknowledge yours.

- Call him, don't text. If you want to avoid another ignored text message, you might want to pluck up the courage to call and say hi. Sometimes a random phone call out of the blue will be enough to remind him of the great time he had on your first date, and if the conversation goes well you will be arranging to meet up again soon. You don't even have to have a specific reason to call him. Do it at the weekend, and just say you were lazing about in the sun and thought you'd call to see what he's up to. The conversation might lead onto you both linking up in the evening for a casual drink!

- Text or call him ask a relevant question or for some help in his area of expertise. Sometimes you can trick a guy into a second date by asking for his help on something. For example, if he is handyman, tell him you want to put a shelf up but you don't have an electric drill. He will probably offer to do it for you, and at the same time you can thank him by preparing a casual lunch – *and there you have it, your second date!* It might not seem like a good idea to trick someone into having a second date, but personally I think at this stage it is okay, because you are still both deciding whether or not you are compatible, and some people are less open to things and need a bit of casual encouragement.

Texting doesn't have to be just for teenagers. It can be a useful tool for taking things to the next stage.

Section 2

Making It Exclusive

Confidence is Key

Congratulations! You have found an attractive man with long-term relationship potential, you have gotten him to notice you, had a great first date, and now you are dating. The next step is to take your man officially *off the market*, before some other women gets her claws into him!

I know that sounds somewhat on the possessive side, but you can't afford to be lapse, this is your future, and the potential love of your life we are talking about. It is your job to make sure that he knows your relationship is exclusive, and that it's not okay to be dating other women. If you don't establish where you stand with him, you won't be on the same level, and may be unaware that he still considers himself to be footloose and fancy-free.

Tip…

Most men won't mind making things exclusive with you, if they think you're worth it. Men only shy away from commitment when they feel there might be something better out there, or if they feel they might be losing something in the process.

How do you make him want you, and only you?

I have three words for you – *confidence is key*! A woman who questions herself will be questions by others, but a woman who exudes confidence will make the people around her feel secure too.

If you want your man's eyes to be focused on you, and you only, then you have to show him that you're worth looking at. And I am *not* referring to the way you wear your hair, or do your make-up.

Men are interested in women who are strong and independent. They are more likely to chase after the time and attention of a woman who has her own friends and life, and feels comfortable being her own person.

For starters, this is the kind of woman who has lots of interesting things to talk about, because she is living her life to the full, she is self-motivated and is passionate about her own ambitions and personal interests. Do you know anyone like this? Don't you find them exciting and inspirational? These are the people others want to be around.

Remember…

If you are needy, or spend too much time chasing after your man, you will give him nothing to work for, because you are readily available, telling him about everything that is happening in your life. If you retain your independence on the other hand, and keep a bit of mystery about yourself, then he will have to work harder to find things out about you, which will feel *much* more satisfying to him!

In order to pull off the "Independent Woman", you need to be *confident* in yourself.

What is a confident woman?

- A confident woman knows who she is
- A confident woman knows what she is good at
- A confident woman knows what other people think about her
- A confident woman knows her own flaws, and makes them work *for* her
- A confident woman knows what makes her attractive to other people
- A confident woman knows what she wants and how to get it
- A confident woman knows she deserves to treated right
- A confident woman knows that a man does complete her
- A confident woman knows how to balance her work life, social life and love life
- A confident woman knows it is okay to make mistakes, because that is the only way to learn

Did you notice that in every single one of those points is the word "knows"? Confidence is all about knowing and approaching everything which realistic optimism and positivity. If you *know* that there is a possibility you will fail at something, it should only make you more determined to succeed, because confidence is also about not being afraid.

If you want your man to accept that you are the fabulous woman he wants to commit himself to, then you have to be confident in the fact that are this sort of woman. As soon as your confidence improves, so will his desire to have you for himself. He will sense the confidence you have in who you are and what you're worth, and he will realise that he could lose you to a man who is willing to give what you deserve, so he will make the decision that he wants to be that man, and he will make it exclusive.

Why you shouldn't push exclusivity onto a man

It can be tempting to try and nudge your man into committing to you, but in doing so you will be showing him that you are not in fact as independent as you make out to be. A woman that who places pressure on a man to confirm the exclusivity of their relationship is a woman who *needs* a man; and this goes against everything the *independent woman* is all about!

If you want to know where you stand with a guy, yes you can ask him straight out if he is still dating other people, but make it because you want to establish a balanced relationship; and if he is dating other people, that means you have the option to do that too.

Don't freak out if he says he isn't ready for exclusivity and that he wants to keep dating other women. There is no point on placing pressure on a man if he isn't ready, it will only push him away. A man needs the space and freedom to realise of his own accord how special you are.

You can't tell a man what he wants. What you can do though, is show him that you are not needy, by accepting that he is not ready; but also show that you are not going to waste your time waiting around for someone who is not one hundred per cent into you.

I'm afraid you will have to do a bit of bluffing until he changes his mind about you, but it will be worth it. We will explore this next…

Show him your fun side

So you are dating a guy, and you're not exclusive yet, but you want to be. You know the guy likes you a lot, you have a lot in common and you have a great time together; but he just isn't ready to commit.

Firstly, well done for not latching onto him like a leech, being needy and revealing all of your insecurities. Every woman who really, *really* likes a guy and doesn't want to lose him before they've even *got* him will feel a sudden pang of desperation if the guy is displaying signs of not being ready for a relationship. It is only natural to feel this. But you can pat yourself on the back for holding those emotions back and remaining casual about things, even if it is only on the outside. Believe it or not, you are one step closer to a proper relationship!

Why should you be cool about him not committing to you?

- He will be impressed that you haven't gone crazy on him. Most girls who are really into a guy would have lost their cool if a guy admitted he isn't sure if he wants to be exclusive just yet; but if you managed to take it gracefully, and you have shown you are emotionally strong, and that it hasn't put you off him completely. He is more likely to sit up and pay attention now, because he can see that you have a healthy level of self-respect, which is independent, self-confident and sexy. Plus, he knows you don't *need* him. **Note:** Just because you have accepted that he isn't ready to commit, it does not mean you have to take part in an open relationship. You should hold back on allowing the relationship to develop sexually until you know he is ready to be exclusive with you!

- You have just made yourself into the challenge he is craving, because you have shown that you are a strong woman who doesn't need a man in order to be happy. The weird thing is, that now he knows you don't need him, the emotional responsibility has lifted and he is soon going to start wanting you to care more. But you're not going to give him that satisfaction of course, until you know he is ready to commit to you fully.

- Once he realises that you are now available to other men, his male instinct to compete will fire up, which only means more attention for you. He is going to have to work harder now to get your interest pointing in his direction, and when it finally does, it will feel like more of an achievement because he had to work for it! Playing hard to get with a guy isn't about sending mixed messages; on the contrary, it is about being blatantly clear at what the situation is. You like him, but you are confident enough to know there are other options available, so you don't *need* him, and you don't necessarily *want* him if all he going to offer you is a casual fling that any of the other guys could also offer, if not more!

What can you do to entice him more?

Now is the time to have some fun! Show him what he's missing out on. Keep giving him tasters so he knows that you're still interested in him, but hold back on the good stuff. The good stuff is reserved for the men who take you seriously enough to make things exclusive. You won't need to tell him that of course, but he's not stupid and he will sense that you are holding back because you know he won't commit.

As soon as you reveal more of the fun side of your personality, and as soon as he sees that other men are drawn to this side of you, it will up the stakes and erect a nice ticking clock.

How can you reveal your fun side?

You don't have to stop dating your man, but you do have to change the way you behave on your dates. Here are some ideas that will make him sit up and pay attention.

- **Be carefree in your approach to dates from now on**. This means, don't get emotionally involved, and don't let the tone of your rapport with him go beyond fun and flirtatious. Never talk about your feelings, because that will render you vulnerable and exposed; instead have fun and focus on enjoying the moment.

- **Don't be immediately available when he asks you out.** I'm not saying you have to be shady, go ahead and tell him if you have arranged another date or if you are just feeling a bit tired and fancy a night in. Whatever the reason is, standing up for your own availability will show him that you value your own time, which will make him work harder to make it worth your while the next time he suggests linking up.

- **Don't focus all of your attention of him**. A fun girl to be around is a girl who enjoys simple pleasures, like having a laugh, hanging out and doing nothing in particular and going to places that she finds genuinely inspiring. If you spend all of your time together staring into his eyes, you're not really giving him anything to work for. Transfer your attention into a gift by spreading it to all of the things in your world that make you happy, and soon he will want to be one of those things, and will work harder to make you happy!

Tip…

A great way of revealing your fun side in a casual and non-committed kind of way is to invite him out with a group of friends, and suggest he bring people along too. This way he will be able to admire you interacting with other people, and he will see how much other people like and get along with you!

Here are a few ideas for social gatherings you can organise…

- **A barbecue**. If the weather is great and someone you know has a great back yard, this is the perfect, casual and inexpensive way to bring your friends together, and introduce them to the guy you are interested in. Seeing you amongst your own people will make him see you in a different light, it may even get him thinking about what it would feel like to be part of your group of friends if he were, say, your *official boyfriend*! Getting along with your friends brings him one step closer to you, so take advantage!

- **A fun day out in the park.** Bring food, a Frisbee and wear a bikini top if it's nice and sunny! Playing games is a really fun way of bonding. And he will leave at the end of the day feeling happy, with all those feel-good endorphins surging through his body from the physical exercise.

- **Casual drinks in a local pub**. Get a big table, and invite plenty of people down after work for some well-deserved beverages. If it is towards the end of the week, everyone should be feeling ready to let their hair down. The best thing about mingling with lots of friends in a bar is that you don't have to stay talking to the same person all night. You can move around, join in other people's conversations, buy a round and basically just get stuck in! It's a great way to show off your social skills in a laid back environment that gets more relaxed the more people drink!

Avoid the Friend's zone

The only risk in socialising the object of your desire with your platonic friends is that you and your man could potentially enter a danger zone – also known as *the friend zone*! Once you enter the *friend zone* with a guy, it can be near impossible to get out. In fact you may even end up having to deal with the fact that he will only see you as a mate, while he starts to chase one of your gorgeous girl friends. Disaster.

The best advice you will get on getting out of the *friend zone* is to not let yourself fall into it in the first place!

What is the friend zone?

You will know when you have fallen into the friend zone because it feels like the most frustrating place to be on the planet, when you really like a guy!

In simple terms, the *friend zone* is when one of you doesn't feel the same way as the other. If your man has decided that you are a friend, then he won't allow himself to "*go there*" when it comes to any romantic or sexual feelings. You will end up kicking yourself for being too easy to get along with, and you will spend ages trying to figure out what it was that you did to ruin the potential spark you thought you felt between you.

On the other hand you may have made the mistake of slipping into a *friends-with benefits* situation, in which there may be a very strong sexual attraction being acknowledged between you, which is great, but he has already decided that it's '*just sex*', and therefore refuses to let any romantic feeling enter your relationship, which is bad. A guy who is in this sort of friends zone with you is unlikely end up as anything more, unless he is the one who wants more from you, and you are the one who is holding back from commitment.

If you think you are in a *friend zone* of some sort, ask yourself the following questions to confirm the worst…

1. Are both of your emotional needs being met, or is one of you holding back?

2. Are you both getting what you want, and need?

3. Do you both feel good about your relationship? The *friend zone* never feels good, for at least one of you!

4. Does your relationship feel fair and equal? Do you both feel satisfied?

Remember…

Don't sell yourself short. You are worth more, and you don't deserve to settle for less than you really want.

Why does the friend zone happen?

The friend zone is like a place where your guy can't really see you for the attractive and sensual person you really are. Maybe he is mistaking you for one of the lads because you make him feel so comfortable around you? Maybe he is overlooking your emotional needs because you have given him the impression that you don't have any? Maybe you haven't presented him with enough of a challenge and so he has settled for friendship because he doesn't feel he needs more from you than that?

Essentially there has been a miscommunication somewhere, and it has probably stemmed from your own behavior or approach. Here are some checkpoints to make sure that you don't end up in the friend zone.

- **Never forget that you are a WOMAN!** You might be easy to talk to and have a laugh with, *like the lads*; you might be low maintenance, *like the lads*; and you may even have an overly carefree approach to your appearance, *like the lads* – but you are *not* one of the lads. Don't ever let him mistake you for one, and as soon as it happens put him in his place and make him feel like an idiot for taking you for granted.

- **Remind him of your femininity and sexuality.** If you are worried that you could be entering the friend zone, quickly give yourself a makeover and remind him (*and yourself*) that you are a woman. It's not about trying to impress him or make him go gaga over you. It is about asserting your femininity, for yourself. Don't do it just for him.

- **Reveal your vulnerable side.** Sometimes being an independent woman can go against you, especially if you are in danger of entering the friend zone. Men like to feel useful, so show him that you need him for something. It might make you feel slightly vulnerable to ask for his help, but this is a good kind of vulnerable, and it will make him warm to you. If you have an emotional problem related to work for example, ask if you can discuss it with him. He will feel honoured that you trust him enough to ask for feedback, and it will make him feel good when he helps to make you feel happy again. Playing a part in your happiness like this can also bring him closer to you and strengthen your bond.

- **Don't pretend that you are invincible**. If he has done something you don't like and upset you, don't just take it on the nose; be upfront with him about it, and he will learn to be more considerate of your feelings. Once he realises that you have feelings and that you will stand up for how you feel, he will think more carefully about how his behavior affects you. This means he is thinking about you on a deeper level, which will inadvertently bring him closer to caring about you.

- **Never forget to challenge him.** A man will quickly become complacent if you are always there. Don't let him take you for granted, make him work for your time and attention.

Are you Girlfriend Material?

The funny thing about relationships is that they can teach you an awful lot about yourself! You can discover brand new boyfriend-inspired interests, and that your personal tastes are more adaptable than you thought; or on the other hand you can discover that you are not girlfriend material at all!

What is girlfriend material?

A woman who is *girlfriend material* is basically a woman who knows how to be in a relationship. She knows the importance of equality, patience, flexibility and communication. She also knows how to make a man feel good, without neglecting her own needs within the relationship and outside of it.

To help you think about what makes a great relationship between two people, and to work out whether you are girlfriend material or not, and decide which areas you need to work on – here is a list of some of the universal qualities that will make you a great girlfriend.

You are independent

This is something that we keep coming back to, because it is so important. Men will get much more satisfaction from a relationship if their girlfriend has her own life and friends. If you are needy, your boyfriend will end up feeling smothered and annoyed, which will lead onto other problems in your relationship. Don't let your boyfriend feel he has to take care of you all of the time. Not only will he enjoy the freedom from responsibility, but there will also be more room for you both to focus on strengthening other areas of your relationship.

- Make decisions on your own if his opinion is not necessary

- Don't sacrifice spending time with your own friends and family

- Prioritise your own needs when appropriate to maintain a healthy balance

You respect his identity

People need to be able to express themselves as individuals. Just because two people are in a relationship, it doesn't mean that you don't have your own individual personalities any more. You don't always have to come as a "couple".

Don't try to mould your man into something he is not either. You should appreciate who he is, and whom you fell in love with, and stop trying to change all the things about him that irritate you, or that you think could be improved. Give him space to be who he wants to be, rather than who *you* want him to be. He will always be the same person underneath it all anyway, so really you are just wasting your time, and causing rifts in your relationship.

You don't nag him

It can be very frustrating when you don't feel you are being heard, or that things that annoy you are not being addressed. The problem is that as soon as you start to *nag* him, you will effectively lose all sense of real communication.

Nagging is not communicating. It is one-sided venting. It usually involves pointing out all of his flaws, and bringing up everything else that bothers you at the same time, in one big rant.

Men tend to be well attuned to the nagging tone of voice – it is something they picked up very early on in life, probably from their mothers. As soon as you start to nag, you go from being sexy girlfriend who he loves and respects, to a nag, just like his mother. It's not an attractive comparison.

Great girlfriends know when they are nagging, and they rein it in. Save your issues for the right time, and communicate your feelings properly, with a focus on resolving the issues, rather than just venting.

His friends and family love you

If you can hit it off with the people he loves most, then you will quickly *become* one of the people he loves most, if not the *person* he loves the most! In fact, guys often use friend and family events to test the waters and find out if you are girlfriend material. He will usually trust the instincts of his friends and family first, so if they warm to you, then he will feel confident in you too.

It is important to be able to develop a good relationship with them as well as with your partner, and this includes being able to talk to them to resolve disputes. If you can't do this, then you become the outsider. Don't be left on the outside – nuzzle your way in and be one of them. He will love you more for it.

You can be the sexy 'girl next-door'

The *girl next-door* is a woman who is able to be her self, and has a natural beauty that shines through in her personality. The ultimate girlfriend also knows how to be sexy and mean it! If you know how to turn your man on because you pay attention to his likes, and his and dislikes, rather than just relying on your body to do the work, then you are a keeper!

You are intelligent

A woman who knows her own mind is very attractive to man. You don't have to *know* a lot about things, but if you know how *you feel* about topics that are being discussed and can hold your own in a debate, then a man will respect and admire you.

Intelligent women have their own opinions, and can also encourage their partners to think in different ways by providing an alternative perspective, rather than always simply agreeing with them. Men will appreciate this and find you all the more interesting and challenging for it

Try it...

There are plenty more things that make you girlfriend material, maybe you can list a few, or bring the topic up with your girl friends over drinks. It can be fun to find out what different people think the perfect girlfriend or relationship is, and you can learn a lot by listening and observing other people's behavior and points of view.

When is the right time to have sex?

You will probably sleep together before you officially decide to become exclusive. Often sleeping together can be the defining factor in making your relationship exclusive – but only if you have sex when the time is right!

If you have sex too soon, you can risk *premature relationship sex failure*, which is where a guy has gotten what he was initially chasing after and immediately loses interest. Never forget that men feed off the challenge a new woman represents, and once that challenge no longer exists, neither does the relationship.

This is very confusing territory, because it is incredibly hard to know whether a guy will go cold on you after you sleep with him. All men are different, and you have to trust your own instincts. If in doubt, wait a little bit longer. The more time you give him to get to know you on a real level, the more time he has to form an emotional bond with you.

You may think you have no control over this problem at all, but there are some things you can consider while deciding on whether it is the right time to sleep with your man.

How do you feel about the development of your relationship?

Stop trying to figure your man out for a minute, and look inwards at yourself. It can be easy to forget that your own needs are very important in this situation, and is not all just about trying to avoid scaring him away!

Ask yourself the following questions to get a better idea of how you feel about the development of your relationship.

1. **Do you feel good about yourself?** If the relationship is a good one then it will make you feel confident and glowing. There won't be any niggling insecurities, and you will feel strong within yourself.

2. **Do you have lots of other things happening in your world?** It is important to feel like you are leading a balanced life, and that sleeping with your new man is not the main thing that you are prioritising. If it is, then you risk taking the whole thing out of proportion and over-thinking things. When you obsess over anything relationship-related it is never a good thing.

3. **How much importance are you placing on sex?** Why does sex have to be such a big deal? Okay, understandably, women tend to invest a lot of emotion in having sex, especially with someone new. But have you ever considered that if you were more casual about sex, and didn't necessarily link it to love, at least not at this stage, then the stakes wouldn't so high and it wouldn't be such a big decision to make after all? Why not sleep with him, because it feels good, and it feels like a natural progression? That's as good a reason as any.

4. **Do you feel you know him well enough?** Sleeping with a new partner is very intimate, and it can help to make you feel more secure if you are sure that you know enough about him before you go all of the way. If you realise that you don't actually know much about him at all, even if you have been dating for quite a while, then hold out, and focus on creating intimacy outside of the bedroom – talking on a deeper level can bring you a lot closer together. Try sharing some personal experiences with each other, and see what you can learn about him that way.

How do you know if you are ready for sex?

It might have been a while since the last time you slept with a man. Sex with a new partner can be a bit like opening up a can of worms if you rush into it. You should always make sure you are ready to make the next step, and you can do this by being honest about what you really want.

Having sex with a new partner is not a way of dealing with your insecurity of him losing interest. Neither is it a way to keep hold of a guy just because you hate being single. Don't have sex to feel better about yourself, and don't have sex to make a guy like you more.

If you are ready for sex it will be because you feel aroused whenever you are around him, you feel safe and not needy or insecure, and it feels natural and you are ready. You should never have sex for the first time with a guy for any other reason.

If you feel it is right, just go for it!

Presumably you are an adult of consenting age, and so is your guy; so if you feel it is right and you want to take your relationship onto new and exciting territory, *go for it*! You can easily avoid any first-time sex anxieties by being responsible and wearing protection. If you know that you want to sleep with your guy, it can be a good idea to make sure that you have condoms in your purse – never rely on a guy to have them.

Always be independent and keep condoms on you. Otherwise you will have to cut your sexy session short, which will pout cold water on the whole thing, and place pressure on the next time you get together, because you won't know whether to presume that you are going to have sex, and you might both feel a little awkward, not wanting to make assumption in case the other person is offended.

How do you let him know that you're ready?

There is only one simple answer to this question, and that is, to take the lead! It will be even more of a turn on for him, and no man is going to get mixed messages if you kiss him with the intention of wanting it to go further. It's like a male instinct, they can sense when you want to go all the way or if you are holding back, so simply *don't* hold back!

Impress his friends & family

As we have discussed, getting along with your man's friends and family is a must if you want him to truly accept you as a girlfriend and make it exclusive. So how exactly do you go about impressing them, and what effect can it have on the growing relationship with your new man?

Always be yourself

Getting his friends and family to like you is a big deal, and meeting them for the first time is likely to make you feel very nervous, because it is so important to you that you make a good impression! Unfortunately when you want something so much that it produces nerves, you can end up trying too hard.

One basic giveaway that you are trying too hard is when you try too hard to be someone you think his friends and family will like, even if it doesn't ring true to your own nature and personality.

This is a big mistake, because *your guy already knows you*, and he will sense immediately if you are being fake just to fit in. What's worse is that his friends and family will also sense it, because being false is pretty much transparent to anyone. So you are not going to go down too well.

The best thing to do is to be yourself. Don't focus on trying to live up to anyone's expectations. You will impress them more if you show that you are a genuine person, even if that means revealing that you feel a little bit nervous. They will understand, and they are more likely to warm to you, and bring down their own barriers if you are as honest and natural as possible.

The great thing about being yourself, is that you will feel comfortable in your own skin; and when you feel relaxed, the better part of your personality will naturally shine though, and people will find it much easier to bond with you. If you can show that you confident in yourself, other people will feel confident in you too.

Don't do anything to make anyone feel uncomfortable

Remember that these people don't know you yet, and so whilst it is preferable to be as natural as possible, it is also wise to be on your best behavior. Don't do anything that will make his friends or family feel like they shouldn't be in the room!

For example, any heavy petting or kissing is *not* advised. A peck on the cheek, and holding hands is about as far as you should go in front of his friends and family while you are still getting to know everyone. Anything more can come across as a bit too possessive or intimate.

You don't want to make your new man feel uncomfortable either. He will find you much more attractive in this situation is you can demonstrate the *independent woman* part of your personality. He will love to watch you interacting and getting along with the people he loves. So rather than cling to on to him, go ahead and mingle.

You should also avoid being too opinionated, or bringing up personal issues in conversation. It will be much easier on everyone if you keep the challenging debates until you are all a lot better acquainted. Bickering with your new partner or displaying any developing rifts will also make observers shift awkwardly in their seats.

Don't flirt with them

It's never a good idea to flirt with his mates, or worse his brother, or even worse his *father*! Some women find it easier to get along and bond with other men when they throw in a bit of flirtation, because it shows that they are fun, easy-going and sexy. But if you do any of this when getting to know the people who are closest to your man, he is not going to be very happy at all, and they won't be impressed either.

You don't want to do anything to make your partner feel threatened. He probably won't see it as you just trying to get along with everyone, and get people to like you. He will find it offensive and take it personally.

If his friends flirt with you, it is best to direct your flirtations back towards your partner to show them that you are one hundred per cent into *him*. He will love you more for it, and feel more in control. His friends will learn to respect you too.

Try to be as agreeable as possible

His friends and family will be observing you closely, and if you show any sign of boredom, or complaint, or don't seem very engaged with conversation, you will be labelled as a *bitch*.

Friends and family are only judgmental because they care about him, and they are not doing it to be cruel. In fact most of the time you might not even be aware of what they really think of you because they hide it so well!

Don't give them the chance to label you though. Be as natural and friendly and agreeable as you can, and avoid erecting any barriers. These people only want to get to know you so that they can feel happy that you and your man are right for each other. If you make it easy for them you will be one of the gang before you know it.

Be willing to muck in

The more you can demonstrate that you *belong*, the sooner you will be accepted into the fold. This means helping out in the kitchen when his mum is preparing food, helping his little sister with her assignment, and playing video games or watching the football with his mates.

Section 3

Keeping Him Committed

Is He Mr. Right?

At this stage, you have met the family, got in with his friends, and you are officially *exclusive* – but it is still early days, and you want to make sure that this guy really is the right guy for you before you start thinking ahead into your future together. Now that you know each other well, it is the right time to revisit this question – *Is he Mr. Right?*

What should you be looking for?

If you want to know if you have found someone truly special, who you are going to be happy with for a very long time, there are certain things to look out for in your relationship. Once you have been together for a few months, you should be able to notice areas where you are not so compatible, and whilst these things aren't necessarily anything to worry about, it can be useful to watch out for patterns of behavior that might end up being the root of bigger problems in the future.

I am not saying that you should pick your relationship to pieces and be too particular about achieving perfection, because that is unrealistic, but it is always good to keep your eyes open so that you are constantly learning more about *yourself* in relationships, and adapting.

Here is a list of things to look out for and think about:

- Do you spend the majority of your time together feeling relaxed and happy; or resolving *issues*? If you are working too hard to be happy together and find it difficult to accept each other for who you both are, then you might not be right for each other.

- Do you have enough time for each other? If one of you or both of you work a lot, this may end up interfering with the intimacy between you in the long run. Is this something that you are both aware of? Are you both fully in tune with each other's needs?

- When you fall out, do you have blazing rows that are not really productive, or are you able to wait until you have both cooled down so that you can resolve issues in a more caring manner? Are you able to listen to each other? How good are you both at communicating how you feel about things?

- Do you both have well-balanced lives, or is your relationship all-consuming? A lack of balance can be unhealthy as you may end up relying too much on each other for happiness, when you should be finding your happiness from a variety of different sources. Emotional independence is very important in a relationship.

- Are your routines taking over in your relationship? Routine and organisation is good but there also has to be a healthy level of spontaneity, otherwise you could risk losing the spark in your relationship fairly quickly. Predictability can make you feel secure, but it can also make you feel contained and bored if you don't achieve a healthy balance.

- Do you both have your own lives outside of the relationship? It is also important that you don't spend all of your time being together *alone*. Going out with friends and family can provide a good balance, and it allows you to spend time together with other people around. You will feel and behave slightly differently around other people. Often you have to make more of an effort in social situations, which is good for your relationship, because it gives you both the opportunity to see the other sides of your personalities that you find attractive.

- Do you bring out the best in each other? If two people are right for each other in a relationship they will keep each other feeling inspired and motivated, support each other through problems, and be able to provide comfort and stability.

- When you communicate with each other about problems in your relationship, is it with care and concern, or based on judgement and criticism? Ask yourself whether you are with someone who wants to nurture you and help you grow, or someone who wants to suppress who you are and change you?

- Are you satisfied sexually? Sex is a really important part of your relationship, and even if all the boxes aren't currently being ticked, you should still be able to feel that there is lots of room for development, the closer you become. Are you able to communicate in the bedroom? Do you both understand, or want to understand how to give each other the right kind of pleasure? If either of you are not being fulfilled in the bedroom it can add pressure to other areas of your relationship. Make sure that you both care about each other's sexual enjoyment.

Remember…

Mr. Right is not *the perfect man*. Nobody is perfect, and if you think they are, then you are not being realistic. But finding a man who is *right for you* is possible if you are *true to yourself*. High expectations kill relationships.

Being realistic and flexible on the other hand allows you to give a guy a real chance at making you happy. Happiness is a two-way thing though, and you need to put as much effort into your relationship as he does.

Mr. Right is a man who you can be happy with, and build a future with.

Common Mistakes to Avoid like the Plague

When you get to the stage where you know you have found a guy who fits you, and you know you want to build a future with him, you might find yourself bombarded by a wave of insecurity!

What if everything goes wrong? What if I mess it all up? What if this is all too good to be true? These are the thoughts that run through most women's heads when they can't believe that they are actually in a happy relationship. You mustn't let these thoughts take over though, because they end up destroying what you have already achieved. You have achieved your happy medium, everything is moving at a natural place and everyone is feeling good. But maybe you are not used to relationships feeling good?

There are a number of very common mistakes that women make when they feel this stab of insecurity during the *happy period* of their relationship. Luckily they are very easy to avoid.

Don't get clingy!

You have worked hard to maintain your *sexy independence*, and a stab of insecurity can undo all of it, if suddenly you find yourself feeling emotionally needy. Don't fall into the trap of latching onto your man like you are afraid of losing him. Latching onto your man is not a way of expressing how much you *love* him - it is a way of expressing your fear of *losing* him.

Tip...

You are much *less* likely to lose your guy if you continue to be that *independent, sexy woman* he fell in love with. Guys need space to be themselves, and the more you cling onto them because you want to get closer, the more you will end up pushing him away as he backs off in order to achieve breathing space!

Don't panic if your guy seems distant

Men go through cycles in a relationship, and the most common mistake women make is to pay too much attention when a guy has gone into his own little bubble. Just because a guy has gone into his bubble, it doesn't mean that he doesn't want to be close to you anymore. He is just hiding out and taking some time to *find himself* again.

Being in a relationship can make you feel claustrophobic if you feel that you have lost your own sense of identity because you are a couple. Guys suffer from this regularly because of the levels of testosterone they have in their system. When they spend a lot of time and start to feel close to a woman certain feminine hormones increase, and testosterone, which is what makes them feel like a man decreases. They need to find ways to re-establish their masculine independence, and putting some emotional distance between you and seeking space to do manly things again, helps to balance things out.

If your guy seems distant, the best way to deal with it is to let him do his own thing. If you chase after him, trying to find out what's wrong or force intimacy, he will only back away at a much faster rate. If however you don't chase, he will come back to you naturally in his own time.

In fact he will come back even faster if you demonstrate that you have your own life and aren't affected emotionally by his distant behavior. It shows him that you don't need him, and when you are not around him, he will miss you and come looking for you!

Tip...

You should think of your relationship like you are two people each pulling on opposite ends of an elastic band. If your guy is pulling away from, you, don't panic and go after him, because you will lose the elastic force (attraction). Instead pull away from him too, and he will quickly spring back, just like an elastic band does!

Don't let your relationship become boring!

The main risk in long-term relationships is predictability. The more you get to know each other, the more predictable your relationship routines become. It s important to keep things feeling fresh by breaking out of your usual routines every now and then, and try to keep each other guessing.

Keeping things fresh in your relationship will also make you feel better about yourself. You will feel less *stuck* and more proactive and inspired. Also, experiencing new things together every once in a while will help to strengthen your bond, because shared experiences create shared memories, which anchor two people together and make the relationship feel much stronger.

Don't rely on passive-aggressive techniques during disputes

There is nothing more infuriating in a relationship when your partner doesn't play an active and productive role in resolving disputes. Passive-aggressive techniques do not help to bring you and your partner closer together, because they do not allow for clear and equal communication. If you refuse to communicate openly with your partner then effectively you are not allowing him to communicate with you either, and that is not fair.

Passive-aggressive techniques can include…

- Conveniently "forgetting" to do something that you don't want to do, instead of talking to your partner about how you feel and coming to an agreement *together*.

- Being late intentionally, in order to indirectly assert yourself and take control when dealing with a partner who is controlling. You may have learnt from a young age that confronting a controlling person face to face doesn't work, but that you can make yourself feel like you have more control over things by slipping round the side to do things your way, with passive aggressive behavior.

- Withdrawing emotionally during conflict, because you don't necessarily want to face up to how you are feeling, but you need a way to express it. Shutting off from your partner may feel like you are taking control of how you feel, but actually you are merely punishing your partner without letting them understand what the problem is. This can be an easy passive-behavior habit to slip into, and also one of the most destructive, as it wedges an emotional barrier between you and your partner that can only become bigger.

Passive-aggressive behavior usually comes from people who don't like confrontation and would prefer to keep the peace, but because the behavior means that the person is unwilling to express his or her true feelings, it will only tear a relationship apart.

Look at your own behavior and try to be honest with yourself if you don't want to risk losing your man later on down the line, when it will really hurt!

Getting Him to Commit

If you want your man to commit, it helps to define exactly what it is that you want from him. The term "commitment" has a bad reputation because it suggests that in order to commit oneself fully to one thing, one must give up something else. When you look at it in this way, committing to a relationship can feel like something else is being lost, which is not a good feeling.

So when you approach your guy with the idea of wanting him to "commit" you should really have a good idea of what it is that you want to change. As far as he is concerned, the relationship is great! It is developing at a natural pace and he is happy and enjoying all of the time you spend together. If you drop the *commitment* word into the conversation, he is going to assume you want him to give something up, or change something about the way he lives his life.

What do most women mean when they say they want more commitment?

If you have been dating for a while, and you have now established that you are in an exclusive relationship, suggesting that you want more commitment from your man sounds like you are not satisfied with how dedicated he is to you and the relationship.

When women want a man to commit, what they usually mean is that they want more *attention* from their man; they want their man's *priorities* to be more focused on the relationship, and they want to feel like the relationship comes *first*.

The problem is that if you tell your boyfriend that you want him to spend less time with the boys, less time working, and more time showing you that he is serious about you, he is probably going get an instant headache trying to work out how to juggle everything to make you feel happier.

How realistic are you being?

Of course, you can't expect your boyfriend to give up his life completely and focus on you and the life you are building together, because that's not fair, and it's not altogether healthy either. Every man, and woman for that matter, needs to be able to have his or her own space in a relationship.

Consider the following points to think about whether or not you are being realistic about how "committed" you feel your boyfriend should be to you.

- Is your resentment of him spending time with his friends more about you feeling *jealous* than left out? Perhaps this jealousy is stemming from some kind of insecurity about your relationship? Are you afraid he doesn't love you enough? Think about whether you need to redefine how you think of "love".

- Do you feel that you are doing more for your relationship than your partner is? Perhaps this stems from the fact that you need to spend more time doing things independently outside of the relationship, to make it feel more equal? If you focus on making time for the things that you enjoy outside of your relationship, and develop your own personal interests, then you will be less judgmental.

- Is your desire for him to "commit" coming from frustration caused by the feeling that your relationship is not going in the direction you want it to go in? Perhaps you have already thoughts lots about what you want in your future, and you are impatient to get there? But it is important to move forwards at a pace that is right for *both* of you, and in order to establish that pace you need to talk to your partner about how you both see the relationship developing.

Making sure you are on the same page

If you want your partner to commit, it will only really work if you are both at the same stage of you relationship development. Pushing a man into deeper levels of what you consider to be "commitment" will only serve to push him away. You don't want to give him any reason to not want to be in the relationship, and if he feels like he is on a train that is going too fast, or in the wrong direction, he is going to want to jump off!

You have to get to where you want to be step by step; it is a gradual process. Relationships develop much more smoothly when less attention is paid to the various levels of commitment that take place. If you can let things happen naturally, everyone will feel more comfortable and happy.

If you feel your boyfriend needs prompting though, you can define to *yourself* what it is, specifically, that you are not happy with; and then work on resolving each issue one at a time.

Remember...

When you communicate properly with your partner, you are much more likely to find yourself on the same page. And if you are not on the same page, at least you can both see your different approaches and you can work together to bridge any gaps.

Quick tips for getting him to commit

- If your guy is a commitment-phobe and doesn't want to be in a relationship, then don't give him the *benefits* of being in one! Make him see that actually being in a relationship is a *good* thing, and allows him to get much closer to you and feel much better about himself.

- Never dish out ultimatums – this will *not* make a guy want to commit to you. You need to show flexibility and be fair if you want him to *want* to commit!

- Show him that commitment turns you on! If he sees that more commitment from him only means great things, not only for you but also for him, then he is more likely to want to give it.

- Don't ask for commitment straight up. As long as he knows you're only going to get serious about a guy who is serious about you, then he has the choice as to whether or not he wants to be that guy.

- Make him feel special. A guy will really value a woman who makes him feel unique and amazing. If you focus on making him feel good about himself, rather than inadequate for not making you feel happy, he is more likely to work towards making you happy of his own accord. The better you make him feel about himself, the more he will feel that he needs and wants you to be in his life for a long, long time. You will become part of who he is, and how he views himself.

- Remember to pull away when you want him to sit up and pay attention. Don't let him take you for granted. I don't mean go off and sulk – instead simply start paying more attention to other things in your life. Give him the space to miss you and come looking for you. When you do this, you will enable him to realise how he strongly he feels about you, and what an important part of his life you are.

Men always tend to shy away from "commitment", so never mention the "c" word. But be clear about what you want from him and if he loves you, he should naturally want to work hard to make sure you get it!

Make Him Head over heels for you

When you are both happy in your relationship you will see the best sides of each other! The best relationships are based on good times, happiness and laughter, because it is during these carefree moments that you will be able to see what you love about a person with a tremendous amount of clarity.

If you want your man to fall head over heels in love with you, give him plenty of opportunity to see this happy-go-lucky, carefree side of your personality. Put all of your focus into creating good energy within your relationship and it will grow into a happy, healthy and strong one.

Be the best girlfriend, and friend you can possibly be

Prove to your boyfriend that he made the right choice to be with you by being supportive, motivating, proactive, fair, and the magic word – *happy*! The more you can show him how happy you are, the more he will feel he is doing something right. Every man wants to be able to make the woman they love happy.

If you spend most of your time complaining, or trying to change things about your relationship, your boyfriend will constantly feel like he is inadequate. He may even begin to feel like he doesn't deserve you because he isn't able to do the simple thing of making sure you are happy.

You can take all of that pressure off him though, and take responsibility for your own happiness. Here is how…

1. When you feel down and things aren't going the way you had hoped, try to avoid blaming your boyfriend, even if

he does seem to be the cause of things not going the way you want. Try instead to think about what *you* can do to alter things in a way that will make you feel better.

2. Remember that you can't control the way someone else thinks and behaves, you can only communicate to them how you are feeling and what you think. What you do have control over is your own thoughts and behavior, so use them to bring positivity into the relationship, instead of letting your negativity fester and grow out of control.

3. Don't rely on your boyfriend to make your life feel full or complete. Establish a healthy balance and find fulfilment in other areas of your life, in order to take the pressure off your boyfriend and your relationship. When you have a busy and full life that is brimming with lots of different things, you will appreciate the time you spend with your loved one even more!

Put as much positive effort into the relationship as you can

Sometimes men like to feel spoilt too. Make your man feel special by making the effort to do things for him that he will appreciate. Your gestures don't have to be big and flamboyant; the smallest, most mundane gesture can do so much to show that you care.

For example

- When he sits down to have breakfast with you, butter his toast for him as you do yours, or top up his coffee or juice – it will make him feel looked after.

- See him off to the door with a kiss if he leaves for work before you – it will make him feel warm and bubbly all the way to work.

- Send him a message, midday, to let him know he is on your mind. The same works well if you are out doing activities without him. He will feel good to be reassured that he is part of your world even when he is not standing right next to you.

- Pay attention to all of the things that he likes and dislikes. He will feel all the more close to you if he realises that you know him so well.

- Make an effort to be sexy for him and he will feel lucky to have you as a girlfriend – buy new underwear!

- When a guy flirts with you, brush him off so that your boyfriend can see that he is the only one for you.

- Be thoughtful and remember things that are important to him. He will love you more because you he will see that you want to help and support him in everything he does.

- Tell him you think he's handsome if that is what you are thinking when he asks you! A man loves to know that when his girlfriend seems to be deep in thought that she is thinking of him.

Be the best sex he has ever had

It might sound shallow to you, but any man who discovers his girlfriend is amazing in bed will be very reluctant to let her go. Your guy will show so much appreciation to you in all other areas of life if he is sexually satisfied.

You don't have to be a sexual gymnast or know the entire Karma Sutra to be the best sex he has ever had. Great sex is all about having the right attitude. Here are some tips...

- Only have sex when you are really in the mood. Sexual enthusiasm is important, and if you are too tired and not feeling turned on, it won't be the best sex he has ever had.

- Give it one hundred per cent! Show him that you really love having sex with him, and don't be shy about it; he will feel amazing. A man will love you even more for making him feel good about himself.

- Be adventurous and open-minded – let him explore his fantasies and don't be afraid to share yours either!

- Don't be afraid to try something new. If it feels good or appeals to you, go with it. Any man will admire your experimentation and confidence.

- Be creative and keep him guessing. Don't allow your sex life to become too predictable. Be spontaneous and keep the fire between you alive!

Remember...

It doesn't take much for a man to fall in love once he has found the right woman. So make sure you are compatible, and be your wonderful self!

Love for Life

The final question is how do you get a man to want to spend the rest of his life with you? What is it that clicks inside a man's head, and tells him that you are *the one,* and that he wants to settle down with you, and build a future with you? Well, there is no sure answer to this question and it will be different for every couple, but one thing you can rely on, is that if a man has chosen you to share the rest of his life with, then it must mean that he trusts in you completely.

Trust is the key word in long-term commitment

Successful marriages and life partners are not based on "love" at least not in the romantic way that most people think of. Spending the rest of your life with another person is a massive commitment, and the feeling of being drawn to one particular individual is much, much stronger than romantic love.

If a man decides that you are *the one*, it means he *trusts* you to be there for him, through thick and thin. He doesn't consider there to be any risk involved, because he *trusts* that your feelings for him are genuine and real, but most importantly that the bond between you is so strong he can *trust* that no matter what experiences you will both have to face, he will always have you beside him, because he knows that is where you want to be.

Trust really is the glue that brings people closer together, and holds them together for a long time. Close friendships that you have had for many years are based on trust, and so are good family relationships and longstanding work relationships. Even a relationship between two strangers is based on trust – for example if you are doing business with someone, you have to trust that they can provide the services you need.

How do you be the woman he trusts and wants to love for life?

The only way you can persuade him to trust you enough to want to commit to you is to be your self in the relationship, communicate fairly and illustrate that you can provide enough emotional stability in the relationship to make him feel secure. If you show your man that you are able to let go enough to trust him too, then he will feel all the more confident in you.

Here are some of the main things that will show your man you are trustworthy.

- Complete honesty – try to be straightforward, even about the smallest of things and he will know that he can always rely on you for the truth about anything.

- Be logical – If you can recognize the difference between the irrationality of emotional responses to the rational and productive sense of a more logical approach, then you will make communicating with your partner *much* easier. This doesn't mean you don't have to acknowledge how you are feeling though, even when it doesn't make much sense! Discuss your emotions with your partner and he will see that you are easy to talk to and that you want to make things work.

- Express your feelings openly – Don't be afraid to tell your partner when you don't like something, or when something makes you feel uncomfortable. The more you let him in, the more he will get to know you, and the stronger your bond will become.

- Engage in dispute resolution, rather than withdrawing or attacking during an argument – If you use defensive actions, you will only draw a wedge between you both, and your man will not be able to trust in your bond.

Conclusion

Now that we have come to the end of this guide, I hope you thoroughly enjoyed reading, and have absorbed enough insight and information from *The Woman's Playbook* to inspire you to go out into the world and be confident in finding your Mr. Right, and making your relationship work!

What has this book taught you?

You now have the tools to discover what your own attractive traits are, and you can recognize what kind of man is right for you.

You have been given some fun ideas on how to attract his attention and get your first date, and you don't have to be afraid about following up after your first date with text messages or a phone call to arrange another.

You have gained insight into what is likely to push a man away, and how best to approach things when you want to establish exclusivity. You have even found out how to deal with a man who is not keen to commit!

You know how to avoid the dreaded *friend's zone*, and you have decided whether or not you are *girlfriend material*.

You know the importance of sealing the deal by impressing his friends and family, and now you are sure that he is Mr. Right and you are ready for the big commitment.

You know all the common relationship mistakes to avoid and you are well on your way to allowing your man to fall head over heels in love with you.

Most importantly, you know what real long-term relationships are made of!

Good luck in your journey, and receiving the happiness you deserve.

Made in the USA
San Bernardino, CA
21 September 2018